S0-DOO-225

A Packet of Seeds

by Marie M. L. Brinsfield

For Bob

Marie Brinsfield

Vintage Voices

A Packet of Seeds

A Journal of Nature Observed
by Marie M.L. Brinsfield

Brinsfield, Marie M. L.
    A packet of seeds / by Marie M.L. Brinsfield. --
p. cm.
    ISBN 0-9671599-1-1

1. Human ecology. 2. Gardening. 3. Brinsfield, Marie M. L.
4. Nature--Social aspects. 5. Social ecology. I. Title.

GF50.B75 2003   304.2
                                            QBI33-1397

All rights reserved. No part of this book may be reproduced in
any form or by any means, including photocopying, recording, or
by any information and retrieval system, without permission in
writing from the publisher.

Published by Jo Atwater Publications
142 Sanford Avenue Catonsville, Maryland 21228
joatwater@aol.com
Vintage Voices is an imprint of JoAtwater Publications

© 2003 Marie M. L. Brinsfield

Library of Congress
Control Number: 2003108014

Contents

About the Author

Marie M. L. Brinsfield is a native of Baltimore and lived for 30 years in Howard County, Maryland. She earned a B.A. in history at Mount St. Agnes College. After a career of 25 years as personnel director and corporate officer in an international textile manufacturing firm, she pursued a Master of Fine Arts degree in drama at the Catholic University of America, and obtained an M.A. in modern studies from Loyola College in Maryland. She established a video production company and produced numerous historical and cultural documentaries, including "Diamonds in the Surf" about beach treasure hunters. Her docu-drama "The Last Day of the Old World," aired on PBS and was reviewed on national newscasts. The film, based on oral histories collected from survivors of World War I, was premiered at the Maryland Historical Society in 1979.

As a freelance writer she has written numerous features for the *Baltimore Sun* and for business, church, and garden magazines, including *Garden Design* and *Fine Gardening*. Since 1993, she and her husband have lived at the Charlestown Retirement Community in Catonsville, Maryland where she writes a "Nature Notes" column in the monthly in-house publication, *Sunburst*.

Acknowledgements

These writings have appeared in somewhat different form in *Sunburst* and were inspired by work with Charlestown's Nature Trail committee and, certainly, by the view from my window of the property's handsome urban forest. These essays have been well-received by the residents and, because of this encouragement, I have collected them, with some additional commentary, in book form.

The book would not have appeared without the professional editing and publication by my sister, Jo Atwater, whose reputation as a teacher of writing persists at Charlestown, and the patient pre-reading by my husband, Jennings Brinsfield.

Foreword

The strongest roots of these essays lie deep in the passages of childhood, seeded by the roving interests of a father who took me along on Sunday excursions into meadow and wood, pointing out the mysteries he had discovered on his job. He worked outdoors as a cartographer, inspector, and buyer of rights-of-way for Maryland highways. His job carried him to then undeveloped rural areas: to Washington Boulevard; the mountains of Boonsboro in the far west of the state; and later, to World War II NIKE sites where he served as an agronomist, writing specifications for the surrounding greenery. If he had had his way, we would see black-eyed susans along all our highways.

Along the way he was an intent observer of the natural environment. He did not hold my hand as would a parent, a mature role he played uneasily; I was along as his audience. We tramped along, him talking all the while: no deep thoughts, just re-discovering his earlier finds; focusing on the tiny and absorbing the whole; stooping low to marvel at miniature mushrooms red with black polka dots; climbing the hill above Gwynn's Falls; wading among mayapple parasols; sometimes flushing rabbits. We sat on the running board of the old Chevrolet eating lunch and watched a trap door spider excavate his home. Such findings don't come out to meet you; it is a habit of active looking that leads to the pleasure of discovery.

At other times he brought his finds home: a chameleon from Western Maryland that turned silver when we put it into a tin pan; a box turtle saved from death as it crossed a road blinded by the urgency of nesting; a live baby rabbit bought for a quarter from a country boy in Scaggsville. Some treasures seemed to find him. Once, an owl came to roost in our Christmas tree left overnight to lean against our back fence. He said it came in the tree that a farmer had given him on a right-of-way, a likely tale. A mature praying mantis, blown by a gust of autumn onto our screen door, was invited in to perform on the top of our dining room buffet. These "show and tell" times were his claim to appreciation, to make up for side-stepped domestic responsibilities. It was what he provided.

The line between scientific discovery and Irish fantasy being genetically blurred, some finds were cloaked in the telling with mystery. He pointed out a low stone igloo in the woods. The house of the Easter Bunny, he said. Already skeptical about any Easter Bunny I let his story go unchallenged. Probably it was an old spring house. A "petrified egg," found in a stream, that he said showed the talons of an eagle around it. It was still among the keepsakes he left behind half a century later. Who knows? Like *Alice In Wonderland*, these tales crossed into metaphor where a found thing could become something else through the looking glass of imagination.

My own early initiatives ran to caterpillars. Fascinated with their plump fuzziness, I patted mud into hedges constructing corrals in an effort to keep them as pets, supplying them with clippings of grass and jar tops of water. Returning to my "farm" under the porch one day after lunch, I learned that they could quickly climb over these fences when I accidentally sat on a fat white one which, to my tearful chagrin, smeared snottily over my dress. But my passion was sustained.

When our first grade class was learning to read we were sent to the public library to select one book of interest. The others chose various children's stories. I chose an illustrated book on caterpillars. Awed by the variety of these creatures' vivid colors and distinctive patterns, their specificity of design, their purposeful camouflage, I searched for meaning. How had this

come about? The wonder remains and has only increased as I get to know the landscape out my
Charlestown window.

In Spring, my father brought each of us a package of
seeds to be planted and nurtured for the summer: Cali-
fornia poppies, sweet peas, snow-on-the-mountain. A
favorite poem came along with the seeds. Only the first
and last couplets remain in my memory but they carry
the nub of the message.

> *"I paid a dime for a package of seeds*
> *A dime was all that I had . . .*
> *A dime's worth of something*
> *Known only to God."*

I treasured a pack of cards published by Coca-Cola. I
think you were given one when you bought a Coke but
Daddy got me the whole pack, courtesy of a country
store somewhere along the highway. Similar to the
Topps baseball series, each card showed a color print of
a different wildflower along with its Latin name and a
short description. Other sets showed insects and birds. I
carried those cards around like any other girl's beloved
doll, shuffled and memorized them, and was delighted
to discover many of their namesakes growing in the
woods and open fields near our neighborhood. I was
marked for life.

During a college exercise in precis writing we were asked to read two stories, "The Riveter" and "The Bee." Each story described in technical detail the working of its principal "character." We were to decide which was the more interesting. I was the only one in the class to choose "The Bee." I think it was assumed we would choose the human worker. For me, it was no contest: a mere riveter catching hot rivets in an iron bucket versus the natural baskets on a bee's knees collecting pollen?

Since those days I have planted numerous gardens. I even had a frog come to live in my house through one whole winter, a stowaway that hitchhiked hiding between a pot of hibiscus and its redwood container brought in from the patio. At first, I noticed a slight movement out of the corner of my eye. Then, becoming bolder as he learned I knew he was there and meant him no harm, the frog hopped about the edges of the room. He once attached himself to the television screen in response to croaks from a like amphibian in one of the Wonderworks stories! "A Froggy Went a-Courtin'?" My frog became a shy companion, my prince, a Lancelot for widowed evenings by the fire, until, alas, having devoured all the mites I had left to flourish on the green plants for his benefit and the tiny spiders under the ledge of the hearth, he passed on to frog nirvana in late April just before I would have sent him out to the patio with the hibiscus.

The years of discovery, wonder and awe have brought a knowledge of self and a one-ness with all living things. How strongly the threads of childhood remain in my head. How fresh the joy of a dewy spider web spread across my window in September. How wide and rich the landscape and how varied the focus, from the exploding universe of stars to the splendid mystery latent in a speck of poppy seed. It is nothing less than our inheritance of Genesis.

Marie M. L. Brinsfield
Catonsville, 2003

The power that makes grass grow,
fruit ripen,
and guides the bird in flight
is in us all.

Anzia Yezierska
"Red Ribbon on a White Horse"
Beacon Book of Quotations by Women

Last Looks

Spring Meadow Drive
October 29, 1993

Birds and more birds came today to our garden: two nuthatches, a pair of cardinals, five goldfinches, a covey of doves, two downy woodpeckers, a solitary blue jay, our regular mockingbirds and house finches, and a flock of juncos and chickadees come for the winter. And five bluebirds. We wished for them in spring and they come in autumn, moving in when we are ready to go. The resident red-tailed hawk rode the thermals above. Our live-in blue heron stood still as marble, alert for movement of an unwary fish in the pond. A tribe of evening grosbeaks stopped for the day to rest, refuel, and check coordinates enroute to who knows where? Synchronicity! We are doing the same, planning our move to

Charlestown; taking a last look, paring down, sorting out, checking details.

November 5, 1993

A fanfare for our leave-taking! As we pack up the last few dishes, we are delivered the First Prize award for "Best Overall Garden" from the local garden club. How can we leave? Looking out our sunroom window we decide we

have accomplished one goal—a "perfect" garden: English-style mixed perennial borders, a
pond, a shade garden, apple and pear trees,
dozens of roses, streamside daylilies, active
wildlife. No, it is easier to close the door and
move on to the next challenging phase of life.

November 7, 1993 7:30 a.m.

A doe and twin yearlings amble through the
garden, clear the fence. The yearlings
scramble through between the lower logs; the
doe sails gracefully over the top of the fence,
clearing the lilies. They stop to drink from the
cool waters of the brook at the bottom of our
garden, look back at us, then cross under the
stone bridge into the thicket and out of sight.
Do they know we are leaving and the green-
sward by the willows will soon be theirs and
they can nibble the rhododendrons at will?

November 10, 1993

We open a new door. Brookside 117. Fresh white walls and carpet, unshaded windows wide to the woods beyond, aglow with the palette of autumn; yellow of tulip poplars, coppery-gold of birch, deep red of black gum, earthy brown wood chips on a trail beneath. There is a wishing well below our window.

How propitious
for our wishes!

Just above our windows, another signal. An abandoned hornets' nest hangs from a branch of dead wood. I am wooed back to the time my father brought me such a papery specimen. It was his kind of gift. I took my trophy to show the third grade.

I am home. And I will know this place, for life is of a piece and home is where we are.

Genesis

Seeds—what a mystery they are! Even the ones small as a speck of soot contain the makings of next spring's flowers. That such a tiny bit of matter can transubstantiate itself into a specific design—a black-eyed Susan, a Mexican rose—is a miracle of what we call "Nature." Such a power-packed seed might lie underground for centuries and, when disturbed by a searching archeologist, a bit of warmth, a drop of water, will awaken it to life—a new life to grace the liturgy of beauty on our planet.

Our astronomers and astronauts have surveyed some of the planets in the galaxy we call

our Milky
Way and have
seen nothing
like the gentle
verdure of
Earth. The
secret of
our Eden
lies in the
heart of that
seed that will
sprout up green
next spring. It is
the secret of us. We lie at the
propitious juncture of time and
space, that hallowed orbit in the universe which is the altar of the life we know of,
and we, the living creatures—plants, animals,
and man—its sacraments. How can we not
love and nurture the unfolding mysteries of
our garden?

Timekeepers

"It's time!" whisper the clouds of white asters piling up along our roadways in "October's bright blue weather." They are fluffing out the veil of autumn coming down the aisle. Asters are among the timekeepers. Their blooming clocks the length of day. We have several kinds, most of them white, some woodland varieties, some sunlovers. We have the tall New York purple aster, too. The Maryland yellow aster thrives in September along the Old Frederick Road just as one enters Ellicott City. It has already played its quarter and set seed.

The ubiquitous chrysanthemum, in its many varieties, is a timekeeping crew, too. Nothing like them to cheer up the waning season even on drizzly days. "Get ready," they are telling us, for pumpkins, hot vegetable soup, and cleaning out the fireplace.

Timekeepers, too, the leaves are tapping down their green chloroplasts, exposing the colorful chromoplasts that have been there unseen—by human eyes, at least—all summer while the green chloroplasts have been busy turning moisture and sunlight into the tree's food. Now they will strut their colorful seasonal parade. "Get ready!" It is time for autumn leaves to claim center stage. Just after a rain, the sun shines through the reds, golds, and oranges, lighting them like lanterns at a garden party. The sky is festooned with a full spectrum rainbow. This is the glory Florida retirees mean when they say they miss the change of seasons. We are lucky to have it.

Autumn also has its mission in the earth's renewal. Fallen leaves enrich the soil for the following year. Later, the cold of winter will scarify perennial seeds to prepare them for early germination in the Spring. Seedlings, germinated in late summer, take this time to grow strong roots to support new growth and blooms next year.

We of a certain age have come to our glory season, too. The talents we earlier subsumed to our work and responsibilities can come through. Volunteers have time to work for others. Latter day artists find time to paint or create poetry. We all find time to enjoy new friends. Now, we have time.

Survivors

For special reasons, we concentrate at this time on survivors, messages of the durability of life, especially of humankind. This season summer is also a survivor, still vital into mid-December.

Around our doorways winter kale, its queenly ruffs as crisply pleated as Elizabeth I's—deep purple, lavender, pink, white, and variations in between—its lacy frills nestle into every shade of green. Because of their color variety, winter kale can be planted into designs, stripes, circles, even monograms. Kale is definitely a survivor and will remain fresh deep into winter cold. Once in Alaska I saw heads of cabbage, kale's shyer sister, as big as beach balls, growing in a community vegetable garden alongside a wooden church.

In Alaska, too, gentle pansies courageously survive and thrive, their blooms growing to the size of a man's palm. Their laughing faces even brave the icy wind in planters set on bows of tugboats trolling Juneau's harbor. Pansies double up with varieties of winter kale in planters around our campus. A striking combination of purple, pink, and white kale with tangerine-colored pansies greets visitors at one doorway.

More tenuous is the longevity of the geraniums which still survive in protected—and not so protected—spots around our neighborhood. Plots of them still brighten the lawns of the Basilica in downtown Baltimore. These are upstarts, holding their perfumed botanical breath, along with the delicate impatiens, whose days are surely numbered.

Reflecting, our December this year is more

like the balmy climate of the ancient middle east and so more truly in keeping with our various religious celebrations.

May the peace and good will of this holy time of our calendar be a lasting survivor.

Marie Brinsfield

What a Beautiful Morning...

We awoke to the icy curtain of winter. The rising sun poured its rosy glow on glistening trees. We looked out as from a balcony in the universe. A thousand diamond eyes gleamed in the hushed theater of winter, as if awaiting the *grand jete* of a giant Nijinsky.

Less mystically, the scene brought awareness of Earth. One ancient oak fell that day in our small forest, its majestic height and protective shade greatly to be missed. But it will lie there still, a host for mushrooms and a shelter for the smaller wildlife of our community.

The thaw dropped chunks of ice to the forest floor and exposed the broken limbs of many trees, their brittle bones weakened by long life and a dry, searing summer. But, in Creation's perpetual cycle of renewal, the ice brought water to sustain the new life seeded just below the surface and refreshing drink for thirsty roots.

Yes, downed electric wires turn off some of the comforts of civilization; man's constructions being, we are thus periodically reminded, no match for Nature's powerful energy.

On such days in winter, while our astronauts search the universe for ice as a birthmark of life on other planets, Nature reminds us that we already have the water of life. Aren't we lucky?

Waiting...

Winter months are the kindergarten of summer. Mother Nature drapes a clean, white blanket over her sleeping off-spring. The cool moisture beneath nurtures roots developed during Indian summer, awaiting the warmth of the sun to announce it is time to awake and greet a new season.

The dry, brown cups of the seed pods on tulip poplars are filled on snow days with dollops of gleaming white, like hundreds of sno-cones on display for those crossing the nearby bridge. One of Nature's winter desserts.

We are at the exit threshold of winter and we are waiting. Sap has funneled down in the trees. Their leaves have been shed to lie on the earth, composting into fresh new soil. Milk-weed pods have burst with the coming of the first frost and flushed their seeds to the wind to waft along on poofs of cotton fluff and settle offspring in their neighborhood. A thick quilt of winter snow would be welcome now, its warmth and moisture to nourish the life in the womb of winter. We are waiting.

We, all living things, have a covenant with Creation. Spring will come. Its memory is in us. As modern humans we can call its image forth at will. Archeologists speculate that ancients were not so sure if spring would come, or when. That is the reason they built Stonehenge and the Mayan temples. Even the pyramids are thought to have been built in reference to the Sun, light and shadow on their planes of stone read as keys to the natural progression of the seasons of time. Though we wait, we know the season of new life will come. We are waiting.

While we turn up the thermostats in our structured environment, some birds and animals are off to a warmer climate, or hibernating in dens. Their circadian rhythms, too, dictate the cycle of seasons. They know, by a more intuitive sense than we do, that spring will come.

Flowers and trees, like us, wait in place. The earth hugs their seeds in the lullaby of winter. Perhaps that is why we are thrilled to discover their tiny early blooms in spring, like newborns come to affirm that life is ongoing. Meanwhile, we wait—and celebrate—entertaining the angels of our season.

But wait! I hardly believe my eyes. Here in the cold, still forest, the bare bones of trees casting long shadows across the path, there is excited movement. Among the dry, brittle leaves that remain on the beeches, birds flit back and forth seeking, investigating, then rooting about among the chips on the trail. Their swift, graceful movements are not those of the resident crows that regularly hold loud conventions in the woody arena, expounding on one thing and another from their pulpits in the treetops. These are the characteristic flittings of our chirping red-breasted friends, the vanguard of Spring. I declare to myself: These are ROBINS!

Herbert Run, shallow from weeks of dry weather but gurgling into December, now in the first week of January is silent, solid and still, its foam frozen into crusty white collars around the dark rocks. The thirsty robins peck about through the thin ice but stop to sip only briefly hopping about as if they have forgotten their galoshes. One, probably an experienced grandfather, flies up to the lawn near the buildings, hoping no doubt to slurp a few juicy worms warming in the noon sun. It ignores the plump presence nearby, seeming to know that the bloated white giant is only a plastic snowman.

How to explain this earliest of early visits? The daily news is filled with unexpected deep snows and snappy winter weather along the southern seaboard. Their winter vacation spoiled, these robins are moving along ahead of their normal schedule hoping to find emergency accommodations in our Maryland backyards, like families caught in an airport between legs of their holiday trip.

Of course, you could imagine they came back here for the opening of Congress. With their chubby tummies, red vests and brown frock coats they do look a little like bureaucrats. But, any way you look at it, they are welcome.

Meanwhile, some creatures are living on the

edge. Birds on the
wire. I see them every
time I drive aong
Frederick Road. They
are the pigeons of
Catonsville. In times past they perched on the
slate roof of the old bank at Ingleside Avenue,
but now that roost is picketed with metal
spikes to discourage such avian loitering. And
so they have taken up swinging on the wires
crossing the bridge over the Beltway. Why
there? I asked myself often as I passed. Because, I've concluded, there are warm thermals
rising from the, albeit polluted, river of traffic
streaming below. Their roost feels toasty these
cold blustery days.

I recollect my childhood pleasure, standing
over the open grate in our downstairs hallway,
my school dress ballooning with the heat blowing up from the pipeless furnace in the cellar

below. I shivered, sucked my teeth, and sighed with warm relief as I dropped my books from school. I smile at the amazing persistence of such a slim memory.

Birds keep warm by clustering together, sometimes meshing their feathers to increase the insulation. Even species that are generally loners, tuck in with kin on cold winter nights. One investigator found 36 bluebirds in one birdhouse!

Finding food is an adventure. I spotted Becky, a close relative of Bushy the squirrel, devouring the red berries on the hawthorns. I had thought these hard little berries were left this late because they might be poisonous. To birds, maybe; but Becky was having her little fists full, stuffing them in as fast as she could, her tail vibrating with gluttonous glee. The branches on one side of the tree were stripped

bare. "Go, Becky!" I said aloud as I passed.

And there, on top of the mulch in our mini-garden plot, lies one of the Emperor tulip bulbs planted only this fall, dug up no doubt by Bushy himself. Ugh! Unpalatable, he let it lie for me to find and replant, the nub of its first shoots already showing. If the marching ranks of big, red blooms show snaggle-tooth gaps come spring, I will know who the culprit is. Daffodil bulbs are immune to his scavenging because they are poisonous.

Farther along, the grandfather of all squirrels is messing about in a row of crocus shoots, green above patches of melting snow even though the thermometer drips icicles. Cause for hope. Indeed, that is the mission of crocuses. If only Minnie the rabbit spares the blooms, they should be out by Ash Wednesday. Meanwhile, creatures are living on the edge.

January Fun

"Whee-ee!" shouts Bushy, skating down Herbert Run lickety-split past the wishing well. It is a bright sunny, very cold day in the neighborhood. Herbert Run is frozen solid, and Bushy is still a juvenile squirrel. The widely advertised deep, deep snow we were warned to expect over last weekend never materialized and there is no snow cover on the ice, just like the old days on Gwynn's Falls that his great-grandmother told him about.

"Inscrutable humans!" He laughs out loud at his human neighbors hibernating inside, hoarding paper and bread. "Come on out!" he squeaks, zipping to the side avoiding a black rock sticking up from the ice ahead. "They live like they're on a cruise ship," he snickers.

Oops! Bridge ahead. A tributary flows into the Run from a mystery source under the Short Line railroad. The water is warmer there. "Eek!" he squeals. "Past the bridge, I'd be swimming." He does a figure eight around a rock and takes off up the trail. There, in a wider frozen pool, he executes a figure or two for his secret audience, nature watchers behind the windows above who, he knows, are fascinated by his everyday clowning.

Cotsy the rabbit and his growing family are tucked away in the hollow log down the bank from the witch hazel, missing the fun. Hah! Their long, flat feet might be better on a deep snow day, but not in a deep freeze, dry and clear.

And those birds at the pond, they're marooned! Thanks to the fountains they've got that pool of open water, getting smaller every day. Bushy wonders why they don't fly down to where summer went.

"Its a good thing I'm a squirrel," he beats his furry chest in self-congratulation. "I'm smart. I make the best of it. What's a little ice? And what about those laughable puzzles they construct around their bird feeders? What fun it is to foil those contraptions. Ta-ta, I'm on my way. See ya around," he calls skating off, his bushy tail puffed out in the wind.

Reflections

The Mapuche Indians of Chile have a word, "Illequelle," which translates "eyes watching the moon." Flying home from Arizona at 20,000 feet, the full moon was alone with us above a shelf of white clouds. Suddenly, through a break in the fluffy blanket, another moon shone up intermittently from the blackness below. What could this be? A signal from below? The ancient words became a truth: "Eyes watching the moon!"

I did not want to look for reality but to hold the dream of those Native Americans whose pueblo culture I had glimpsed so recently, those women and men who watched nature's signs. A meandering ribbon of silver drew back the veil of my reverie: a river reflecting the moon above. The "moons" below were quiet lakes in the midnight blackness mirroring the light that is itself a reflection of the sun that the ripening fields love.

"Eyes watching the moon," a sacred image from the language of a people who saw the divine in nature. To lovers of language, the repetition of twin syllables perhaps gives a key to its meaning: Ille-que-llen. To analyze its etymology is an intriguing game; to be alive to nature is a grace.

Fog

Fog can be a depressing sight especially in February. Black limbs of old trees, ominous behind the dead white scrim, look like ghosts in the cemetery setting of a Gothic novel. One might expect a cry of "Heathcliff" echoing across some nearby moor. Yes, fog can be eerie.

On a moonless, starless night cruising through the Bosporus toward Istanbul, an all night journey, I squinted out a porthole as we passed Gallipoli. I saw nothing, only pure white as if a damp sheet had been drawn up close to the glass. Without a view of the wake, no motion was perceptible. For long minutes, all was silent. It was as if the ship hung in the air, motionless. Then, with haunting regularity, the ship's foghorn crooned its ominous warning for hours, punctuating the sense that something was "out there," something we were helpless to avoid. At last, in late morning, the minarets of Istanbul appeared.

On a boat trip down the Volga in an unusually warm June, we awoke one morning under a low fog. Because that northern part of the world—just six degrees below the Arctic circle—has a "white night," the sunlight never really leaves the sky. As the hour brightened, we walked to the bow of the boat. What would the sunrise be like? Slowly, then all at once, a completely circular rainbow appeared before us. The sun itself was made more beautiful by fog. The fog of the woodland is a fog we can love. Its softness veils the stark reality of the forest in winter. It suffuses light and makes everything more beautiful.

Fog is a natural beautifier. Actresses like the diffusion of a "Bleckman lens" to glamourize

their closeups. Like an
actress preparing for
her opening night,
Nature relaxes in
the spa of a foggy
late winter day,
soaking up moisture to
smooth out the wrinkles and
creaks of winter. Soon, she will
take up the mirror of March,
brush her vining locks in the breezes of April
and, taking up the wreath and garlands of
May, make her entrance for another season
on stage.

Oratorio

Monks, trumpets, bells! Get ready! Here they come! Usually in this morning-time of year we see hooded brown heads of skunk cabbages poking out of the snow like so many monks at matins in a pre-spring orato-rio. This year January is warm and we have to search for them among the dark, wet leaves.

Skunk cabbages generate their own warmth and actually melt a space around themselves in the frozen earth. Their name is apt; they do have a fetid odor, by design. Holdover win-ter flies, mice, voles—sometimes even birds— are drawn by the scent and scurry under the moist brown hood, helping the cabbage to reproduce by facilitating self-fertilization. We have only two skunk cabbages that I know of on the trail, both in out-of-the-way patches of damp, dark soil. Skunk cabbages even like an occasional flood where there is an underground spring.

At our home in Howard County, Plum Tree Branch at the foot of our yard overflowed its banks yearly after the early thaw and mallards flocked swimming around among the skunk cabbages. Nesting on hummocks, they raised coveys of ducklings. Did these parents choose the site because its musky odor repelled any predator, like the resident fox?

Two other hooded plants will soon be roiling up in Eliot's "cruelest month," April. Wild ginger will huddle close to the ground, and Jack will take to his pulpit to announce, "May is on the way!" Do these early plants have a native wisdom and prepare themselves with hoods to protect their pregnant centers from the early season's unpredictable elements?

Other early
entrants in the
procession are
bell-shaped, the
better to trumpet
Nature's incom-
ing bride, a new
and virgin spring.
Toothwort and trout
lily are two of these. Others, like
Virginia bluebells and wild foxglove, almost
audibly "ring their bells." Spring is here!
Spring is here! Get ready! Here they come!

A Stirring, A Roiling

I lay awake making mental notes about the hyacinth and daffodil shoots pushing through damp brown soil, even while the leaves on the rhododendrons curl tightly with cold. I met a ladybug inside the window glass today. I think the decision is made. The nymph of spring is about to make her entrance.

Then I raise the blind on a Sunday morning and see our woodland robed in puffy white. I have been taken in! February lifted its misty veil just long enough to tempt us with a glimpse of April, then suddenly flung around her the cloak of January's ermine.

It is part of the wonder, not knowing exactly; a glimpse will drive us on. A sudden eclipse will give us pause for contemplation. And so, not weary with the waiting, we are kept keen with anticipation.

These mornings the weather is full of surprises: cool? warm? windy? sleet predicted? It is one of Nature's periods of transition, telling us that nothing is all this or all that. There is some of each season in all seasons. There is a dynamism, a cycle, that is the essence of being. We are never altogether what we were or what we will be.

And no life is ever wasted. The energy of last summer's sun remains in winter's withered, decaying leaves. Instead of raking them away to be discarded we can dig them into the warming spring soil to nourish new plants or last autumn's seeds lying dormant there.

And so it is with us. We experience loss—lose some of our "leaves," so to speak—but then awake, stir ourselves, and begin again, our energy renewed.

Genesis Redux

The earthy breath of spring is not yet in our nostrils. There is a pause in the visible movement of nature. It is a season of great quiet, like a breath taken in. The Native American seasonally went off into the forest among trees, birds and animals to find his own spirit. Now, for us too, it is a time to contemplate. By no accident, it is the season of Lent. We are hushed and waiting.

It is March and, by my calendar notes, about the 25th we will see a golden carpet of lesser celandine on our woodland floor spread for the soft slippers of incoming spring. Then we will let out our hushed breath in a cry of joy. As the sun moves down the northern latitudes, cultures across the globe will celebrate. Alleluia!

It is a time of passage, sometimes bittersweet, when the old make way for the new. At winter's close I have lost two sturdy friends. One great oak, king of the forest, weakened over several seasons, finally succumbed and had to be felled. Its great rings counted the events of 150 years of reign. In another spring, I had planted a wild downy false fox-glove (gerardia virginica) near this oak's roots, testing the legendary mystery of their symbosis. Alas, it too expired, passing along with its patron into botanical after-life. A late winter ice storm—itself a sight of magical beauty—slew another giant oak, vanquished by the sheer frozen weight of the very water it thirsted for in a long sere summer. It fell with a painful roar one afternoon like a knight unhorsed, its upturned roots gouging out a crater in the thawing soil.

But these wrenching events mask only for the moment an array of redeeming virtues. The oaks lie on the forest floor where a season of fungi will rise from their rotting bark, generations of insects and worms will feast on their slow decay, and a fertile compost will nourish the nearby soil. An enterprising squirrel—I've named him "Uncle Wiggly"—has promptly claimed the ancient stump of the kingly oak. He sits upon it nibbling the morning's rummage. A recluse salamander, the first I have seen in this area, has found a lair among the upturned roots of the ice-fallen oak. Startled, crouched upside down and completely still, it is indistinguishable from the nearby roots as I stop for a closer look. He basks in the sunlight let in by the absence of the fallen trees.

Later on, that sunlight will coax out new generations of wildflowers and a generation of saplings in the clearing.

These nights, the March moon is full and shining brightly, a lantern at the window. Spring is tapping at the cold glass. But winter has pressed the snooze button and turned over, pulling the blanket of late-season snow up around her. Ho-hum! Not yet! Not yet!

Crocus leaves stand tall, but their blooms still shiver under the coverlet of mulch. One mysterious bloom, like an upturned yellow umbrella against the March wind, braces near the warmth of a brick wall. A cheerleader come to school too early for the game. No doubt it missed the weather reports, and why not? Wrong as they often are, we might all be caught unawares by the sunshine when we expect a blizzard.

Not so the robins, out in full force. Slurping worms from beneath the brown grass, they more accurately measure the weather, chirping their forecast. "Cheer up! Cheer up! It's coming, we know! It's coming, we know!" The oy-yeh men of the village, they march the neighborhood sounding their fanfare, "It's coming!"

Probably, spring doesn't want us to be too sure, to be too ready. Best be unpredictable; more awesome the surprise, while winter, an old man, lies uncertain in his bed, spring will make her entrance to the harp of dawn and kiss him awake. Then the earth will swell to welcome new birth, a season of renewed life.

Other mysteries: How does an onion know it's spring? Opening my darkened pantry, I find an onion sporting a six-inch crisp green sprout. Life is indeed determined. Does the full spring moon tweak these urges toward fecundity?

It's no mystery how we know when it is Easter. The full moon does govern our Easter date. Our celebration of the Resurrection, the triumph of life over death, is triggered by the lunar cycle. Easter falls on the first Sunday following the first full moon after the vernal (spring) equinox. Thus, its date may be forecast centuries ahead. This year spring arrives on March 20 at 3:03 a.m. EST. At that moment the sun crosses the equator south to north and the day is the same length as the night. And, in that Christian calendar, the third Sunday of Lent is called Laetare Sunday, a day of anticipated joy. It is coming!

Snowbirds

Those three robins we saw in January searching for worms in all the wrong places turned out to be the advance guard for an invasion. They must have sent word back to the flock that there were good pickin's in the woodland around our neighborhood. For, like a bunch of avid tourists just let off a bus on the Interstate, robins have descended en masse. Sightseeing? More likely site-seeking. Some 50 robins rummage for the blue-black berries that might still cling to the ivy on the twin poplars outside our windows. These berries may be tasty morsels but they have been long since picked over by earlier shoppers who left town for the orange groves and Disney World last fall.

Touching, it was, and there was little humor in it, watching these plump brown birds wearing their russet red vests fluffed up against the cold, flutter in uneasy footings on the slim stems among the still green ivy. Generally not seed-eaters, robins don't visit neighborhood bird feeders. Once a woodland species, they have evolved into ground-hopping border birds, accustomed to backyard environments with lawns, gardens, and compost piles where even a casual laid-back robin can cock an ear to the ground, select a delicious lunch, then sip and dip in a nearby birdbath "poolside." Robins have become almost sybaritic in these abundant resorts, offering their "Cheer up, Cherie!" to robin mates and gratuitously to any native people around. But on these snowy days they are silent and nose-to-the-grindstone earnest, holding on for survival.

These visitors toured our woodland for a week or so. We caught them swarming over the landscape hollies near the bridge, devouring berries. Then the snows finally came. The robins were back scrounging the ivy for what they left on their plates the first time. Where would they roost and what then would they eat? Let's hope they moved on to some farmer's barn or a still-flowing streamside where a bit of food could be found.

Its not exactly a rare phenomenon, this flocking together of robins. I've seen them carry on by the dozens, frolicking in and out of a lawn sprinkler in pure playful joy, like children cooling off with the hose in summer. Robins strip dogwoods of red berries in the fall. But then, they are en route to winter vacations to the south. Now, on their way north, the dogwoods have long been cleaned out and the flocking of the robins has the look of desperation.

Others will find and feast on the dark blue berries in the deep winter green of the old ivy climbing the tulip poplar outside my window.

Ivy grows in straight, trailing vines for many years. When it gets old, it begins to "bunch out," blossom, and produce these treats. Like ourselves, in youth the ivy is working on its own ambitions, climbing the heights; then, as it ages, the old ivy begins to reach out to others and produce fruit.

When the robins moved on, along came the juncos and titmice, investigating the ivy. They must be looking for a bit of salad to add variety, for they do get their fill on the ground under bird feeders. This tribe of six or seven snowbirds root about in the three-year-old squirrel's nest, still solid in the crown of a slender beech. The juncos peck away, however. They must have found something tasty in that old nest of brown leaves.

A sapsucker frequently visits a stressed beech tree outside our windows. Tap-tap-tap, he drills holes, releasing the sap, not for his tongue to sip, but to attract insects that will become his lunch. I hate to see that graceful beech go; it will probably not leaf out next spring. But there are several young ones rising up around it. We, and the sapsucker, will enjoy the new generation. As T.S. Eliot wrote, "Everything in its season."

Talk about master builders! That squirrel put that nursery together with everlasting stuff. Not even Floyd's hurricane-force winds dislodged it. The storm knocked down dozens of mature trees, yes, but not Uncle Wiggly's nest. It's an architectural perfection worthy of Ayn Rand. Wiggly doesn't use it any more, of course. One wonders, why? But we watch him—or maybe it's Aunt Wiggly—feverishly building a new home every year. Its almost as if the squirrels don't know they'll need one until the last minute, just ahead of the stork.

Cotsy, our resident rabbit, ventured out in seeming amazement after a heavy snowfall, his footprints tracing be-wobbled patterns on top of the snowbanks at the edge of the woods. But oops! A little way farther on he sank up to his belly, leaving snow pockets as big as a man's boot, and struggled back to the hard-crusted layer near the woods. He scurried along the snow-covered top of a felled trunk and disappeared beyond. I like to imagine he went into its hollow from the other side.

For beauty, on a scale of one to ten, the little snow that came first was by far the prettier. It clung to every twig and in the early morning the woods fairly glowed with the brightness of angels. It seemed to excite the birds who pecked about as if drinking it in like manna from heaven.

A kind of Panis Angelicus.

Send in the Clowns...

Don't worry they're here! There's Uncle Wiggly. Each morning during October he races up and down the birch outside our window, chomping off surprisingly substantial twigs of dried brown leaves, then jumping across to deposit them in the ivy on the ancient poplar nearby. Building what? A nest at the doorway of winter? Is it because the weather feels so much like spring?

The squirrel and the woodpeckers know that the old birch has died. When its caretakers cut it down they found its innards completely hollow. Uncle Wiggly can't believe it. He still shows up early every morning, scrambling onto the log and, quizzically nodding his head, eyeing the deep hole in the stump. What fun for us to watch this unwitting—but not wit-

less—little clown.
"They have ruined
my tree," he seems
to be saying.

And there is the
witch. A surprise
find—witch
hazel! Its crinkled
yellow ragamuffin flowers look like forsythia
blooms that have gone zany. Its hard nut-like
pods can "spit" seeds 30 feet. Witch hazel gets
its folksy name because forked branches
were—indeed, still are in some places—used by
"diviners" to locate underground water where
wells might be dug. Such nuggets of knowledge
were a regular part of the lore brought to our
family dinner table, along with the day's
reporting, and are locked like pearls in my
memory.

Wild Day

What's going on here? Mikey pondered, peeking out from his hideaway in the mouth of the rainspout at a lady in a sun hat passing by. "They're everywhere, all decked out, wearin' green ribbon bows for corsages. Hey! St. Patrick's Day is over!"

Being the tiniest mouse there is, Mikey has never been to Wildflower Day before. "Wild FLOWERS?" He shakes his head in disbelief, "What about ME?"

Never mind, let's see what's going on. Coming from a long line of wily opportunists, Mikey spies his chance. The door is open. Mingle with the crowd. Watch all those big feet! No reluctant guest he, Mikey scoots past a couple dozen pairs of legs, rounds the corner of the porch. "Hey, she's the one," he squeals and

follows a be-ribboned hostess
right through the door and
into the middle of the
scene.

"Lets party!" he shouts in
mouse patois as he crosses the threshold.
"What a sensational entrance I've made! All
eyes on me. They're all agog!" Across the slip-
pery tiles and into the mail room he sweeps.
"Cheezit, here comes one of them with a plastic
cup. Unbelievable! She thinks she'll catch me
in that thing? Ha!" Across the room, onto the
carpet, he dodges a dozen table legs. "Ha-ha-
de-ha-ha! Try and catch me! Feet everywhere.
They're scattering. I've got em on the run.
Drat! No food at this party. Not a crumb.
What's that I hear? Down on the trail?
Punch and cookies down on the trail? What
kind of a welcome is that for a freshman
mouse? I'm gettin' outta here." Throwing his

imaginary cape
around his
shoulders, as if
by magic, Mikey
disappears down the
hallway into the
unknown.

Marie Brinsfield

The party went on as planned. A great suc-
cess. Another sunny April day down on the
trail. Visitors came to see the flowers. And one
tiny visitor from the world of
the wild added special drama to
the day.

I've Got Fan Mail!

*I*t's Mikey responding to comments and a real fan letter suggesting more celebrity appearances and, specifically, an invitation to the pond. April is the month of fools and Mikey thinks he did his share on Wildflower Day. It's made him famous, if not more foolish.

"Hey, the next thing I knew I was chased up and down, skipping though dry leaves and wood chips," he squeaks. An eagle had landed. At least, they said he was an eagle-to-be, a Boy Scout leading a troop of buddies, flanked by a cadre of top brass dads. They came to earn credits, 100 hours, for merit badges and Eagle rank for one of their squad.

"I was not amused," Mikey says, relating his tale from the security of a dry rainspout. The troop had cleared out some of his hideouts and spruced up the place for the visiting "two-leggeds." Mikey scoffed, "April is when they come out for their fair weather airing." And he ran off in the direction of the pond and uncertain adventure. Truth be told, mice can't swim.

April's giddiness gives way to early May and dogwood time. Creamy white dogwood blossoms accentuate the pale green of leafing hardwood trees. Serviceberry blooms are out early as are wild cherry and pear. Vivid pinks of American redbud and Kwanzan cherry rouge the cheeks of spring, while azaleas of every shade flounce about her toes. May brings a warming of the year, settling the skittish weather of April.

Early rains have worked their life-giving magic and the humid air is a mix of flowery perfumes. It is time for queen bees to open their season. One chubby queen gorges on nectar in the tiny blossoms of a redbud out my window. She will soon retire to lounge in sated stupor waited on by her kindred worker bees who will toil on her behalf throughout the summer. Like marketing housewives they will daily visit a succession of fresh-blooming summer flowers collecting pollen in tiny baskets at their knees to carry back to their beloved queen's pantry. As payment they will leave behind the fertilizing dust of pollen to seed a new generation, making their contribution in kind. Thus the "busy bee" does double duty: supplying the honey factory and impregnating a new generation of flowers.

O res mirabilis!

Baby Blues

Around here we celebrate April with a week in the woods. The tiny blue flowers of early Spring, like little French bouquets, are eye-catching above the carpet of emerging green. The "baby blues" of Spring include the Virginia bluebell, blue iris cristata, and the cultivated grape hyacinth, as well as the woodland blue violets.

Color matters in nature. Bees favor blue over brighter yellow, red, and orange. Traveling in Colorado, I learned that mountain flora, especially evergreens, have bluer leaves and needles—the Colorado blue spruce—because the ultra-violet rays of the sun are stronger at higher elevations and blue reflects away the sunlight better than green.

Conversely, the deep green of the forest absorbs more rays to manufacture the necessary chlorophyll.

What's that?! Alas, my reflections are interrupted by a yacking laugh behind me. Aha! It is old Cotsy, bent double, rolling on his back, slapping his haunches. "They did it again! Easter baskets. They actually think rabbits lay EGGS!" (He can't be talking to me.) I hide behind an ivy-covered tree to spy on the scene. It's Priscilla. She's nibbling my pansies! The yellows seem to suit her taste. Oh, stop, I mutter to myself. I just planted them. Hopping over to the crotchety old rabbit, the fusty young bunny twitches her whiskers, batts her lashes over twinkling pink eyes, and provocatively wiggles her cottony tail.

"But now they're getting ready for Wildflower Day again," says Cotsy. "No brown mouse named Mikey is upstaging me again this year! We're gonna stay around, get with the program."

And so they will. Even though we might not see them, they'll be around. Uncle Wiggly will be squeaking about the crowd of "them" coming down the paths, peering at the secrets of nature on the trail which he, of course, believes is his own where he is king, barring the surreptitious nightly appearance of B'rer Fox.

Rites of Spring

"A branch of May I've brought you here
and at your door I stand.
It's nothing but a sprout
but it's well budded-out
by the work of our Lord's hand."

Those words of an old English courting tune learned in college glee club run through my head as April woos May. About the time I was learning that melody I visited a Denver natural history museum. There was a "panorama" replicating the desert in bloom. The vision remained and I planned some day to see the reality, although I was told the blooming of the desert was unpredictable and fleeting, depending upon infrequent spring rain. This year El Nino obliged. I was in Arizona at the magic time to see the carpet of desert bloom—along with a very real rattle-snake sounding an unexpected warning. Another spring another dream fulfilled, another treasure stored in the attic of memory.

In our own back yard the wildflower meadows are all decked out for a ball, dancers in gowns of red poppies, white daisies, and blue flax, all partnered by blue bachelor's buttons and a spate of columbine, some double, in a variety of colors. These, too, are surprises, reaped from a bag of seeds sown last autumn.

Reseed! That's the byword for spring! Bands of spring peepers lend their music as teams march to the field. And the cheerleaders, daffodils waving their ragged yellow pom-poms in the gusty Spring air, are right out front! Sparrows and doves contend for their seats in the stands.

Like survivors of "the greatest generation," wildflowers don't require rich soil to mature; in fact, they insist on growing against odds

and are stronger because of it. They put on
their colorful hats and gayest frocks to meet
what comes with the weather. No superfluous
greenery. Unlike their cultivated offspring the
garden flowers, they require
little care, don't flag in hot
weather nor fall prey to
insects.

Wildflowers are indeed like
grandmothers. They
offer sweet nectars at tea
time to bees who drop by.
They love visits from small
birds who carry away gifts of fruits and seeds,
like preserves they have made with only the
summer sun and rain. And, like grandmothers, they lay for us a quilt of many-textured
hues.

When I was nine, it was a celebration, was
May, like a birthday. Before we sealed all our

Marie Brinsfield

windows and lived our years in air-condition-
ing, we simply shed our winter underwear.
May was the Mother month— sensuous, soft,
palpable. We breathed its perfume; it kissed
our winter-white skin with warm sun; and it
lengthened the days for outdoor play after
supper. At night the sounds of awakening
night creatures, wafting in like moonbeams
through the open windows, soothed our still
early pre-school bedtime. We lay awake imag-
ining animal figures on the ceiling wallpaper.
Outdoors was calling.

Now, one bright yellow pansy plant has sur-
vived winter in the plot under our window. Is
yellow a hardier color? Not likely, the petals,
though yellow, are delicate velvet like the other
colors. What, then? It's my theory that Cotsy,
foraging rabbit friend though he is, has been
dining at the Pansy Cafeteria and he just
doesn't like the taste of yellow. For there are

other pansy plants nearby but they have no flowers, only small green tufts close to the ground. Yes, close to the ground because they've all been munched every time their buds raised their vulnerable little heads; but they were blue, and bronze, and white, and lavender. Cotsy comes around early or late, under cover of gloom or darkness, so we haven't caught him in the act, but the chopped-off stems are there for evidence. There will be more pansies in a week or two, but by then Cotsy will be off to his favorite white clover in the lawn.

As nine-year-olds, we played games wth flowers in May. Buttercups would toss about in the meadows and on neighborhood lawns left long to await them. "Do you like butter?" we

Marie Brinsfield

said, holding a shiny yellow cup under the chin of a playmate, a game played in the afternoons before we swung through the newly-hung screen door and went in to supper. The first iced tea was decorated with a sprig of mint, plucked from the batch planted around the foundation to "keep the ants out." New peas, freshly-baked shortcake topped with juicy Maryland strawberries and real whipped cream. It was May.

May is a time put away the blanket of winter—never a sure thing in April. It is a time to shake out the sheets of spring, open the windows, and hang the screen door to welcome the sweet breeze of May. We are on the front porch of summer.

When May came in those old Baltimore days, Grandma rolled up the woollen rugs, slipped linen covers on the living room furniture, washed every piece of china, waxed all the furniture, washed and stretched lace curtains on long racks in the basement, and got out on the porch roof and scrubbed the painted green shutters. Then she laid the cocoa fiber summer rugs and hung the dark blue window blinds. About the time she served iced tea with supper, she hung the screen doors; summer was upon us.

Those days may be gone, but all the while Nature has been going through the same spring rituals. She has swept away the fallen leaves or steeped them slowly into a new tea for the soil, laid a fresh carpet of tiny woodland wildflowers—mostly pale blues, pinks or whites—and hung the trees with summer curtains of many-tinted greens. The face of the earth is indeed renewed.

It's a mystery that the daintier, tinier, delicate blooms brave the uncertainties of early, early spring. Confident now that the weather will surely be warming, nature had packed away her raiment of April and lays out her summer wardrobe of sun-loving meadow wild-flowers, oxeye daisies, columbine, echinacea. Soon a raid of lightning bugs, like children of a friendly neighbor, will be breezing through the screen door of June to fill the dusk with the fun and games of summer.

As families plan a week or two away at sea-shore or mountain re-creation, some of our visitor birds have come for their summer with us. One titmouse has nested in a cavity on top of a light pole. She can be caught dipping in and out with tidbits—I'm guessing—from the tiny ripening fruits on the nearby cherry tree. Birds are smart; they know which spot to rent with nearby fast food for a demanding brood. That lampost is right on the boardwalk!

May in Maryland! We still have its sweetness:
a succession of flowers; a bounty of greenery; a
variety of weathers. Its a Joy!

The Earth in Being Eaten!!

*I*f we could hear all the chewing and slurping all around us our ears would be bombarded with a continuous "chomp-chomp." For just as we have to eat three meals a day and look forward to dinner, so do the creatures we call wild.

Take rabbits, for example. The one I call Priscilla has started a family and she is weaning her lone offspring, Fluffy, on our pansies while she lolls stretched out under the fringe tree. After the clover has gone under the mower, pansies are most tempting and right there under their noses. Dinnertime for bunnies is early evening and there is often an audience inside going by the windows.

Uncle Wiggly, on the other hand, has an indiscriminate and more robust diet. Who but

Uncle Wiggly would filch a breakfast of cork and sisal drink coasters left on a patio?

A praying mantis came in from the steamy weather to refresh itself on the greenery inside. No telling how he got in. We took him to the outdoors where a lot more good stuff is.

Butterflies sup more delicately, thrusting tiny probing tongues among the petals of flowers to sip nectar. Discriminating creatures, they choose from a definite menu: big yellow swallowtails fancy the zinnias as do the small white admirals; the cabbage whites get heady on the blue forget-me-nots. Baltimore blues pick Queen Anne's Lace. And what were the opalescent damsel flies seeking around the open doors to the swimming pool?

Oh, if we could hear all the insects chewing! We are blessed that our hearing is only a fraction of theirs.

Looking In

The green moire of a jack-in-the-pulpit stands upright and shiny above trailing lacy frills of maidenhair fern. The panne velvet leaves of sage-green, fuzzy with sundew, cling to the woolly brown earth, sharing mottled shade with clumps of violets, their tousles of purple surrounded by ruffs of heart-shaped waxy leaves. Graceful panicles of Solomon's seal nod as if looking down on the carpet of yellow lesser celandine. A pleasing sense of texture comes from "looking closely in." In the seemingly random forest there are elements of design, an unarranged arrangement.

Beside the texture that wakens our sense of touch, nature's color combinations please the eye; no colors clash. In a sunny meadow, crepe paper saucers of orange field poppies toss among ruffled spikes of purple-blue larkspur, complementary colors on the artist's palette. The juxtaposition of their differing shapes form a satisfying composition against a companion stand of bluestem grass. The effect can be striking. Returning from a Fourth of July weekend, a field of red poppies, white daisies, and bright blue bachelors' buttons snapped to attention in the breeze as we rounded the curve toward home. We caught our breath. A perfect holiday salute!

Look
closely
at a
water envi-
ronment. Spike-y
yellow water iris and
stiff brown cattail stand
stalk-straight above the pink
rosette and flat round leaves of
blooming waterlilies. It's natural
ikebana: the iris a line reaching upward, the
"heaven line"; the "man line," a water lily
bloom; the flat round leaves the "earth line."
We reach a state of harmony by "looking
closely in." As easily as breathing, we know
the poetry in our earthly landscape. A promise of Eden. So we might look to an alien eye:
a tapestry of shapes and colors blending in a
natural human community.

Empty Nests

Mid-June the coreopsis was gold in the wildflower meadow. Now, in the early days of July, the flowers are going to seed and nature offers to fulfill a new need. Six or seven goldfinch feast on the ripening seed. Swinging and bobbing on the nodding stems as if on a circus trapeze, the bright yellow canaries flash a new and feathery gold. The performance continues for most of the afternoon. A new amalgam is replacing the old. I stand by to ponder how elegantly the Alchemist works His wonder. It was a double joy that my great-nieces witnessed the magic as well.

In another part of nature's cycle, nests are being vacated everywhere. One tiny empty hummingbird's nest arrived by express as a gift for one of our bird-loving neighbors. A friend had discovered it in Texas. The nests of hummingbirds are, of course, tiny. This one is the size of a quarter and plastered neatly with lichen. Our neighbor describes herself as an "amateur" bird-watcher. The word is derived from the Latin word for love and is thus a league above mere book knowledge or rote. Bless the amateurs! May their genus increase.

It has been said that when grasses set seed, summer is ending. The seed is set. We are still in June, but there are signs of approaching middle age. The trees have shed their graduation garlands and are wearing sedate green. By the Fourth of July our fall chrysanthemums will have set buds.

Mother birds have fledged their young; their mates have shed their flashy waistcoats and settled into laid-back drabs. There is no stronger signal of passing time than the empty nest. The empty nests themselves deserve a closer look. I held a perfect few on my television table for years. Woven like baskets that rival Longaberger, they were sturdy and durable but also beautiful.

Styles of nests are varied and ingenious. The tailor bird actually uses cobwebs to sew two leaves together, first punching evenly-spaced holes along their edges, lacing them up like shoes, and filling the pocket with soft materials. Nests woven entirely of wire have been collected. Appropriately, in Switzerland, a nest was made of old watch springs. Old newspapers are commonly used. Once, in an upright yew next to my garage door, an enterprising robin laid a waterproof foundation to her nest using a discarded plastic sandwich bag. Unique locations are chosen, too. A pair of phoebes had glued their nest atop the porch light of my house even before I moved in. To keep their nursery quiet, I used the back door for that season.

In nest building, utility is the primary factor of place and material choice, but beauty and decoration are evident, too, in the way these feathered housewives "furnish" their homes. Ruby-throated hummingbirds decorate the outsides of their nests with lichen, often using several varieties. Bits of leaves, flower petals, ribbon, and colored paper may be used by other birds. Camouflage? Perhaps. Glued on with saliva and often brightly-colored and in a variety of textures, these decorations are a kind of avian decor. Consider that the bower bird might paint the inside of her nest brilliant blue using berry pulp mixed with saliva and charcoal for pigment and a bit of bark for a brush. She is definitely decorating!

Bless the Wildflowers

There ought to be a blessing for meadows. Certain cultures bless their harvest in thanksgiving; others bless their fishing vessels and fishermen, a practice revived recently in a community by our beloved Chesapeake Bay. A blessing for meadows may just be more subtle a matter of letting nature be. Even the sea grass "meadows" on the floor of our bay flourish when we leave them at peace to seed and grow into lush havens for our precious blue crabs and spawning fish.

On a recent trip down the Volga, a Russian university professor told the story of his marathon walk across America with a group of Russian students They were amazed by the proliferation of America's lawns. "All that good soil going to waste," they said.

Scratch a Russian and you find a peasant who loves the little dacha on its half-hectare in the country, even though he lives out the work week in a crowded walkup apartment in the city. I visited one or two of these country villages of small cottages, much like the little summer retreats that lined our Maryland rivers when we went "down the shore" for relief from the city heat instead of leaving air-conditioned apartments to travel the world.

Behind a rickety fence of unpainted pickets, every inch of land around a Russian dacha is planted with succulent vegetables and beautiful cutting gardens of flowers. The vegetables are mainly for home use or for sale in city markets. The flowers are offered as "gifts" (for a small donation) to visitors from cruise boats stopping along the river. Wild berries are conserved and sold in jars at the boat landing by pensioners in babushkas, along with smoked fish from the river laid out on flowered tablecloths. There is no sign of a lawn along the shaded dirt lanes and wildflowers of every variety grow with abandon everywhere outside the fenced-in plots.

For that matter, there are no more than a few median-strip lawns along main roads through the great Russian cities. Wildflowers bloom among foot-high grasses tossing their seeding tops beneath inner-city stands of fir and birch trees where people walk through worn foot-paths picking berries. To be fair, the northerly climate and short summer season does not encourage vines and thick undergrowth; they do not deal with Japanese honeysuckle and kudzu as we do.

These blessings were so taken for granted there that I was unable to find anywhere a booklet of Russian native wildflowers. Here we have the books, but we mow down our buttercups, clover, daisies and their rarer native friends where only a few years ago they flourished,crowding out crabgrass and dandelions.

Bless them all!

Barbara Walker

I Spy July!

This middle month, named for Julius Caesar, is our American month for explosive celebration. On the 4th the fireworks are of the sulphuric kind. There are bandoliers of firecrackers set off with a touch of smoldering punk, spit devils ground under heels on the sidewalk, sparklers in the hands of children, Roman candles. The history of fireworks goes back to the ancient Chinese who are said to have invented them. Were they only displaying their power or were they challenging the heavens and trying to create stars?

There are gentler fireworks in the floral world, around our doorways. Some are quite spectacular. Take the Hercules clubs. The blooms of these low-growing trees are splendid explosions of white: spreading fronds of pebble-size florets open directly on their treetops like the fingers of a giant hand. They are best viewed from above and we are lucky to have several specimens just below the windows of the bridge. Hercules clubs have no side branches at all and when they lose both flowers and leaves in late fall there is nothing left but the bumpy upright trunk which resembles, of course, a club; hence, the name.

A look-alike is the weedy ailanthus, an escapee from China, known there as "Tree of Heaven" but, conversely, also as "Devil's Walking Stick." Here in America it monopolizes road-sides, inhabits the cindery slopes of railroad lines, even sprouts in sidewalk cracks and neglected alleyways and is sometimes call the "Toothache Tree." Ailanthus was the central metaphor in the novel, *A Tree Grows in Brooklyn.* Its reddish-brown spirals of bloom drop multiple seeds and its speedy growth crowds out all other vegetation. On our campus it takes advantage of ground disturbed by construction which is why we have a bumper crop in the margins of our nature trail.

The fluffy red heads of bee balm, also called bergamot or Oswego tea, qualify as colorful, soft explosions. Native Americans use this plant as a medicinal herb. Its spicy aroma and bright red flower heads attract butterflies and hummingbirds, come to sip their nectar.

The recent rain came, not in the steady dayslong nourishing drenches we had hoped for, but on little pattering feet; but it came and the green is evident again. In the meadow below the bridge the bright yellows and oranges of high summer have given way to the lavenders and purples of perennial ageratum and New York ironweed.

Rain in July is extra warm and a divine

grace for creatures, especially insects. Fireflies are not so plentiful in our chemically-managed world, but on summer evenings they can still be seen, their flashing bodies aglow like a 4th of July sparkler, celebrating their passion for mating. "Here I am! Where are you?" the male flashes. The female, sitting quietly on a nearby leaf, flashes, "I'm here, I'm here! Where are you?"

Go fishing on certain summer nights and follow the glow of phosphorescent life churned up in the wake of your boat, or the opalescent flare of scales on a newly-netted dolphin (not the porpoise kind) as it is brought to the surface. The mounted trophy can never duplicate the fire of those scales. Summer bursts with fire and light in July.

Celebrate!

The Fourth I Didn't Miss

Sick a-bed for this celebratory holiday, I lay sleepless long after midnight, the curtain open to the woods. The fireworks at Catonsville had boomed for an hour or more and then ceased. But outside my window the firefly displays only increased in the silent darkness, pinpoints of white light flitting through the windless leaves in the unabated humidity of the record-breaking heat. Hundreds of them! "Golly!" I whisper aloud, "so many more than other years." My private showing. I watch them until I am lulled to sleep.

Morning, and fireflies have disappeared. Now two immature robins trapeze up and down from fence rail to lawn. Their search for breakfast is challenged by the hard, dry earth.

No rain for
days. "Look
in the
woods," I say
to the win-
dow glass.
"There may
be berries."
Of course,
the robins are smarter
and hop acoss to the patios where the flower
pots hold promise. Then, they hop out of sight.
Alas! But I have had a secret glimpse, a treasured encounter before most of my inside
world is up and awake.

Suddenly, down on the path where an earlier
gully-washer has worn away the chips and the
ground is dusty and bare, along comes
Herman, our neighborly squirrel. Scampering
jerkily—he wouldn't like the phrase—he

sprawls out on his belly and wriggles gleefully in the dirt, up and down, back and forth, feet jutting out on all four sides. "What?" I say. "I never saw a squirrel do that!" Now, he's rolling over on his back "scrooching" back and forth, all fours straight up. A quick turn and he repeats his vigorous routine twice. His morning workout. Suddenly, as if he's seen me spying, he flips upright and scoots up his favorite birch, turning an eye in my direction. Why, I felt he was actually thumbing his nose!

Watership Down...
...a landscape for immigrants

That's what I think we could name our lawn, after the English novel of that name in which all of the characters are rabbits. Perhaps our rabbits' ancestors came to America for a better life. The ones in the book had their adventures. The one on our lawn, that I have named Priscilla, is literally rolling in clover.

It is white clover time and Prissy is treating herself and becoming a bit chubby. Breakfast begins about seven and lasts until nine. Dinner, at about six, lasts a couple of hours more. There must be a long siesta in the cool of the trail between. With food a-plenty there is no sense coming out in that hot sun. I found her tiny newborn bunny—I named him Fluffy—in a tussock of bluestem grass near a clump of buttercups, a comforting choice for camouflage.

White clover wakens memories of bridal parties on Mrs. Zalegaris' lawn. As little girls, we tied hundreds of these tufty blossoms together, making long-trailing veils, and fitted caps of clover for friends who were to be our true future bridesmaids.

Cycles

The natural world moves in cycles, affording us the pleasure of a changing landscape. The cycles move in a sort of spiral as the inhabitants of each season mature.

There is the Head Start School. Early spring flowers get the jump on their later cousins. Smartly, they have stored nourishment in their underground bulbs and rhizomes. At the first degree of warmth they are ready to show themselves. By February, crocuses are blooming and the first chunky heads of hyacinths are pushing above their collars of leaves. Tulips will shortly pop up to carry their blooms like festive balloons above the rest. These are the hardy bulb plants, native to Siberia, Russia, Korea. Over eons they have learned to be prepared for a short warm season, draining

food down from leaves left to die on the plant
and freezing their food underground.

Another head-starter is called spring beauty
(claytonia carolinians). It stores starch in
special short fat stems growing underground
hoarding energy for the narrow leaves and
tiny pink flowers that embroider our woodland in spring like a Laura Ashley coverlet.
The family of violets—there are many varieties—do the same. Summer flowers, on the other
hand, have a much shorter cycle. Seed to
sprout to bloom to seed again and their season
ends.

A much larger orbit paces the life cycle of the
locust (cicada). In Maryland they reappear
every 17 years when trillions of locusts emerge
all at once from hibernation underground.
Then in a few summer weeks they tune up a
scratchy philharmonium, attract mates and
deposit eggs in the twigs of live trees. Soon,

they die and the ground is littered with their corpses, which little boys sometimes find ghoulish joy in dropping down the backs of shrieking little girls. In the Carolinas cicadas appear every 13 years. Is it significant, one scientist asks, that both 13 and 17 are primary numbers, divisible only by themselves and the number one? And, if it is, how do the locusts know?

In a cycle related roughly to the moon, horseshoe crabs, one of nature's oldest surviving species, come ashore at Cape May, New Jersey every spring to mate and lay their eggs. Birds, on their annual migration north, stop to feed on the eggs and move on to their own nesting places elsewhere, one cycle benefitting from another. These cycles are as accurately timed as the moon, by which the feasts of Easter and Passover are forecast, their dates published on religious calendars for centuries into the

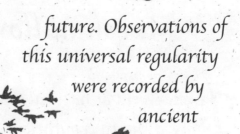

future. Observations of
this universal regularity
were recorded by
ancient

Egyptians,
Arabs, and the
Maya. Our cycle of years
obeys the natural orbit, as   well.

Reassuring in their dependability, these cycles
foster an optimistic look to the future, an
"all's right with the world" attitude. Mysterious and intriguing in their origin, no crystal
ball is needed. We can the more relish the
now-and-then surprises.

Marshmallow Sky

In the world of natural phenomena clouds have a shady reputation. We dub them "ominous," or "threatening," or "somber" and sometimes blame them for our outlook on a gray day. But clouds do their best to beautify our world, as the first astronauts found to their awe when they glimpsed from outer space "the big blue marble" that is Earth.

Clouds are silent metaphors, like the images I used to see, gazing myself to sleep, in the ceiling wallpaper of my bedroom: a soft white lamb, a running fox, a Santa Claus, a bear.

There can even be metaphors in the spaces where clouds are not. When I wished hard that clouds would disappear so we could go to the beach, my grandmother would say, "When you see enough blue to make a Dutchman a

pair of breeches, then it's going to clear up."
If I watched long enough, the blue breeches
yardage eventually appeared. Then, the thin
pale rays of the sun would halo out from the
edges of the clouds as if to spear the earth and
Grandma would say it was, "drawing up the
rain." Then, presently, we could go to the
beach.

Why, the beauty of a sunrise or a sunset does
not even exist without clouds! Thin wispy
clouds, like pulled cotton balls, cast the light in
pale yellow; thick dark gray clouds laden with
water tinge the sun's splendor deep violet; and
there are all the shades of red and orange in
between. Out in the open West, the sunrises
and sunsets nearly surround the horizon with
a gorgeous palette and turn the nearby mountains to dramatic oranges, reds, and purples.

Even the reflections of clouds add beauty to

an already beautiful scene. A pleasant day beside our pond is more pleasing when puffy clouds reflect in its watery mirror, their images playing hide and seek with the growing cygnets and their doting parent swans. At night, a full moon lights a brighter path for kit foxes poking in unknown clefts to learn the ways of their world when there are a few white clouds to increase the lumens. Sometimes, if you listen, you can almost "hear" the moonlight as clouds move across it like sails on a lake. At least, those of us who lie awake mesmerized, do.

Taken as a gift from our natural order, clouds can be deeply contemplative sources of strength for us. Life just isn't as beautiful without them.

An Understory Story

Think trees in the forest: tall yellow pop-lars (liriodendron tulipifera) with their tulip-like blossoms; giant red oaks (quercus rubra); leafy white ashes (fraxinus Ameri-cana.) These are our senior trees, their long spreading branches shading the forest floor beneath. They drop their seeds in disorder to incubate scions of their own kind for a new generation. But by the providential order of nature there is a healthy competition that nurtures cultural diversity. Stretching up-ward for the sunlight, the seedlings of these great trees have to compete with a lower strata of great versatility and variety; these are the understory trees, the juniors of the forest. And among them are some interesting bloomers.

There are the paw-paw trees (asimina triloba) growing in small groves with schefflera-like broad palmate leaves. This American native bears inconspicuous purplish-brown bell-shaped flowers in May, followed in late summer by irregular, cylindrical-shaped aromatic green fruits that turn first yellow and then black. Now that's variety—in shape, scent, color and in taste—for the fruit has a soft, silky edible pulp, which gives it the popular name "custard apple." To taste it, though, one must outwit squirrels and wild turkeys who sense the height of its ripeness and relish it. Our native Americans, who watched more closely the habits of their wildlife neighbors, harvested paw paw fruits to make a yellow dye from the ripe pulp. Custard apples are not now distributed commercially but there is a PawPaw Society, founded only in the 1990s, which aims to broaden appreciation of the shrub-like tree and promote a renewed commercial use of the fruit. They may turn up soon in a farmers' market near you.

Among the native American trees found in the wild by Colonial botanist Bartram is the Franklinia (franklinia altamaha) which grew, in those earlier times of pristine forest, under the taller trees in the damp soil of the South. It is not to be found in the wild now. Bartram planted a specimen in front of Benjamin Franklin's house in Philadelphia and named it for the Founding Father. Franklinia is a stunner. Blooming late in summer, its creamy white five-petaled blossoms with their deep orange centers display themselves against the foliage just turning brilliant autumn colors. Franklinias are planted now as landscape specimens and several thrive at the moist edge of our woodlands where caring hands can keep them free of invading exotic immigrants like strangling Japanese honeysuckle and bind-weed (also called, for ample reason, mile-a-minute vine.)

Sourwood (oxydendron) also retains its panicles of white lily-of-the-valley-like blooms until autumn paints its nodding leaves a vibrant red. Once paddling across a lake in a forested preserve in the hills of Tennessee, I saw more nodding sourwoods and taller than any I had seen elsewhere. Resplendent in their autumn dress, they were mirrored in the lake as if admiring themselves before a harvest ball, while wild ducks of several breeds glided in and out errantly teasing the ripples in their stately reflections like children finger painting.

Flowering dogwood (cornus florida) is a more familiar resident in the lower apartments of our forest. In May its spectacular white blossoms gleam in the dappled shade of the taller trees just coming into full leaf in our Tidewater area. The dogwood is the state flower of the state of Virginia. A ride through their forested highways in spring tells us why. Their white blossoms gleam in the filtered sunlight.

The petals of the dogwood are not its flowers at all. These are bracts, colored leaves, designed to attract pollinators to the greenish center that is the real flower. What a trickster nature can be in the interest of continuing Creation! In their bract design dogwoods are like our Christmas poinsettias whose red petals are bracts and its green-yellow centers are the flowers.

By autumn the dogwood's leaves turn deep red and the pollinated flowers produce brilliant crimson berries. One late October in Howard County, I watched a flock of 20 or so robins strip a dogwood of berries in the space of an hour, gorging themselves before their take-off for migration to their winter resort down south. The few berries that dropped in the mulch sent up sprouts the following spring, so the dogwoods still proliferated.

Among the earliest bloomers in the understory forest is American redbud (cerci canadensis), sometimes called Judas tree or, because of its tiny red-pink blossoms, pee-wee. Redbud likes the forest edge. Its slender branches reach out along roadsides or at the edges of clearings. Blooms cover every inch of its dark branches before the leaves even bud, getting ahead of rivals, attracting pollinators to its pea-like flowers, feeding clans of early-arriving bees. As the blossoms fade to mauve, distinctive heart-shaped leaves arrive to shimmer like aspens in the lightest of breezes. Redbud is an attractive vase-shaped tree, but short-lived. Progeny is assured by pea pods of seeds carried by birds or dropped in the detritus at its base to sprout the following spring.

Weeds

Because we embrace the seemingly ordinary, people often ask wildflower enthusiasts, "What is a weed?" In Ireland recently I learned that around Killarney, rhododendron is considered a weed. Some of the school children there spend their summers in the cool mists of national forests hacking out giant stands of this acid-loving shrub, prized in the garden landscapes of America. Thus, there is no intellectual definition of a weed; it is characterized by its behavior.

A weed is a selfish plant, consuming all the surrounding nutrients, invading the space and destroying the habitat of others. (Hmm, all too human?) On our campus, we have some wild flowering plants that are considered, in this environment, to be weeds. The sweet perfume of the lavender Canada thistle is pleasing. It attracts bees for pollination, but it crowds out all its equally beautiful, but less aggressive, neighbors. Japanese honeysuckle is another aromatic predator, like the thistle an import. The seductively named jewel weed, loving our deep, moist stream side, overwhelms the more delicate woodland plants. (It even tries to bribe its way by exuding a remedy for poison ivy itch.) Crown vetch, the pink ground cover that highway builders plant all over Maryland, blankets many of our slopes to the extinction of wildflowers like Queen Anne's lace, and even our state flower, the black-eyed Susan.

Our canopy of trees is not immune. When our soil was disturbed for necessary construction of our great place to live, weed tree seeds lying dormant in the soil took advantage of new moisture and sunlight and staked out spaces for themselves. Black locust trees threaten to become the tyrants of our border areas and a new generation of the admired paulownia (princess) tree is behaving like a weed and tapping at our windows.

There's a lesson in community behavior we can learn from weeds.

Ah! Bright Wings

In September, the full moon—that porch light of the heavens—will welcome the traipsing parade of autumn.

The woods is getting ready to say goodbye to all the campers of summer: the monarch butterflies, though they were few this season, surfeited with nectar of milkweed— on which they feed exclusively—will follow their mysterious aerial route to ancestral forests in Central America. They are not the same individuals who came up this summer for, even more cryptically, several generations have passed since June. Yet they still know the way. (The earliest known monarch was collected in Maryland between 1698 and 1709 for English naturalist James Petivee; it is now in the British Museum of Natural History.)

The azure blue butterflies have spent
their spring and summer sipping cocktails
from dogwood, spice bush, meadowsweet,
willow and wild cherry—all plentiful in our
woods—stopping to lick slurpees of mud kept
fresh by rains. Blues hibernate through the
winter, each housed in its own chrysalis.

The winsome cabbage whites that make their
happy trysts in midair outside our windows
in the summer sun and drop in at fast food
bars of yellow mustard, bitter cress, and garden zinnas, will stay around, too. They love
the woodland's edge and their share of mud.

Some butterflies, like the blues, have clandes-
tine symbiotic relationships with ants. They
lay their tiny eggs on flowers; the eggs hatch
into caterpillars. Ants, attracted by the sugar
exuded from special "ant organs" on the caterpillars' bodies, offer the emerging larva protec-

tion from birds and insect predators. What
these tiny creatures have is awareness, awareness of those "deep down
things" called to poetry
by Gerard Manley
Hopkins. We
may take the
lesson, and
open our
instincts
to the
pure inner call of
our humanity.

Rain
...a drama in three acts

Was it folksy Mark Twain or folksy Will Rogers who said, "Everybody talks about the weather, but nobody does anything about it?" That seems to be the case with our Maryland drought this summer, which has lasted into autumn.

Drought has good sides, as well. Periodic natural wildfires burn off overgrown forests to let in sunlight to newly-sprouting scions. Meadows are rejuvenated when a new season of cool rain arrives. One special effect that pleases weeders: this summer the drought has curbed the plethora of smothering vines that cover some of our native wildflowers. So it isn't all bad.

The telltale tree rings grown this year will one day tell the story of a drought year, but the mature, established trees will live on. Our own inner selves sometimes experience a "drought" year, a time of sadness only to find a new source of growth and beauty as time passes. A new cycle begins.

The rains have come...and welcome. The trees in our woodland celebrate among themselves like neighbors at a block party on the Fourth of July. Their leaves clap together to the tympanous rhythm of raindrops and their green skirts billow to the dramatic dance of winds. They are greeting the storm with joy after a long drought. Our stream tumbles over the rocks, trilling a counterpoint to the whole orchestration. A storm is a kind of natural theatre.

Drenched with a surfeit of luxuriant moisture, the very few closed gentian growing by our stream, have burst into bloom. Many of our Maryland wildflowers love limestone soil and have found our nature trail to their liking. For the same reason we do not have wild conifers or holly which prefer acidic soil.

There is a freedom to the rain that releases a child-like abandon. Once, in the neighborhoods of Baltimore we ran out in our woollen bathing suits lifting our faces to the rain. We trusted its purity, sometimes stretching out head-to-toe in brick gutters along less-traveled streets to let the gushing water flow over our bodies. We had the same excitement as surfers of today who grab their boards when someone shouts, "Surf's up!" Later, as adults, we stood on covered porches exalting in the drama of a thunder-and-lightning downpour. Today, we can stand in one of our Charlestown bridges, high among the trees, watch the swaying treetops and listen to the dancing raindrops on the roof, protected observers.

We cannot get too cocky about what we know about Nature and her works, a lesson humbly learned since last month. A few days after I filed my paean of gratitude that the rains finally had come, she staged her latest tragic opera, a fury of wind and rain named Floyd. At its curtain call some 25 trees had fallen dead in our neighborhood. We, her awe-struck audience, do not shout "Bravo" or call for an encore.

Such storms as this are "reshaping" events. In the quiet that follows, the local natural world reorganizes. The new light that reaches the forest floor invites the sleeping seeds of sun-loving wildflowers to sprout refreshed. Opportunistic parasites like fungi grow on the decaying trunks. Insects multiply and burrow under the dead bark. Guests at this succulent hors d'oeuvres table, newly excited birds arrive to gorge on the beetles, worms, and insects that rush to feast on the trunk. Squirrels and chipmunks examine splintered stumps and move into new home sites. Salamanders find the moisture they love in the turned-up roots. Snags left upright are targets for hole-boring woodpeckers. Forest ecologist Charles Canham said it well, "To an awful lot of organisms the best tree is a dead tree."

But we humans deplore the loss of these great trees of the upper canopy, the stalwart oaks at least three of which have fallen in the battle with nature this year. They may have been weakened by the invasion of gypsy moths we experienced a few years ago; the moths liked

oaks best. Nevertheless, Floyd has indeed reshaped our landscape. Our best re-use as humans will be to chip the small wood and return it to the earth as nourishing organic mulch around our plants.

Meanwhile, life will be teeming in the large trunks, stumps, and snags left in place as the remains of these old trees weather into the earth. Some of these trees are estimated to have lived for 150 years. Their rings have recorded many seasons of drought and many stormy years.

As Halloween approaches we imagine the shrieks of these dead trees as they fell and almost expect to see their ghosts wailing along the trail in the last nights of October, while their living mates array themselves in costumes of brilliant leaves and, maddened by the full moon of autumn, have a last dance under the harvest moon.

Indian Summer

Early mornings a sheer curtain of fog dims the window of dawn. Nature in our temperate zone shakes out its colorful foliage like an Indian blanket, getting ready for its long seasonal sleep. It is Autumn.

Up in the wildflower bed the cosmos still reign, albeit nodding their heads heavy with early dew. But under their wispy green skirts late-blooming gallardia, rich orange red and yellow, lives up to its common name, Indian blanket.

The common names of flowers tell a silent history. Early settlers of our prairie baptized a number of our wildflowers with native American names: Indian-pipe, Indian-paintbrush, Indian-poke, Indian-turnip; not real pipe but Indian pipe, not a real paintbrush but Indian paintbrush. Thus, the return of warm temperatures after a chilling spell was Indian summer.

And it was harvest time. Indians gathered pine nuts and other wild seeds and berries, stored them for the winter and moved down from cool plateaus to warmer valleys. Settlers preserved their vegetables in root cellars. Our berries and nuts are left for the bird and squirrel populations. The hickory nuts and beech nuts are fast disappearing from our trees and the finches have long-since stripped the wild canes of rose hips. No wineberries are left; the robin got those early. In our time, it is these small creatures that bustle about during this reprieve of Indian summer.

And what of us? As we watch Nature pull up her colorful blanket of yellow, gold, and orange, we enjoy the cozy warmth of our own Indian summer.

Stop, Look, and Listen...

These are watchwords for the nature-lover. Being aware is key. A flicker of white amid the dark green cover of ivy and...Ah-ha! an early spring toothwart. A rustle of leaves and a tiny brown chipmunk scampers across the path. A glint of yellow and a bright canary flits flower-to-flower on the seeding coreopsis. The habit of being aware wraps the senses in a kind of surround-sound. Eyes and ears are piqued by habit for what might be around, for many of the wonders of our nearby world are tiny and shy and have to be found.

It is fun to focus deliberately on the small. Lying face down on a beach in summer one's eye can catch the opalescence of a rainbow in a single tiny grain of sand. Touch the plush surface of a fresh windowsill flower. There is a tiny, nappy "fuzz" that gives a petal the iridescent sheen of life that is the "bloom" of the flower. The wings of butterflies in the same way reflect light to give them color as do the feathers of the bluebird. To see and enjoy these tiny beauties of nature we have to be aware, exercise our senses. It is a quiet work, a small effort, but infinitely rewarding.

In Indian Summer, nature reveals a deeper spectrum. The focus is wide now and on color. Leaves glow with the amazing variety of hues hidden under the green veil of summer. Some of the coppers will remain on oaks and beeches, like ladies wrapped in shawls against the winter wind; they will be shed in spring. Berries of dogwood, bittersweet, and hawthorn punctuate the bare twigs here and there. Cooler breezes rustle dry leaves, like fingers sweeping over harp strings. Aware ears hear the music of autumn.

September, traditionally the beginning of the social season, is also the concert season. Concerts, ballets, theater, opera. A time of movement, maturation, and music. Concerts, you say? Open your windows at dusk and listen to the full symphony of sounds in the orchestra of insects coming into adulthood. Many do not sprout wings until now, the time for their mating. "Find me! Find me!" they chirp. Some make their sounds not with their mouths but by vibrating their wings. Others, like the cricket who sits on the hearth, by rasping their legs together. The songs of katydids, the grasshoppers, the crickets, don't blend in melodious phrasing. Rather, they pipe up—from here, from there—to the human ear like the voices of a hundred competing ventriloquists. All together, then in rondo, they fill the softness of late-summer evenings with a rousing trill of sounds.

In her book, *Stirring the Mud,* Barbara
Hurd "conducts" the orchestra of hidden wild
voices in Maryland's Finzel Swamp by spend-
ing half an hour "loping back and forth on
the road, using my body the way a conductor
does his baton." Her movements alternately

set them singing or silenced them. They have been watching her all the while, "holding their throats" on her approach and inflating them after she has gone:

Under the full September moon with its syco-phant dog star, there is theater worthy of the impresario Diaghilev. "Ettonez moi!" they say, "Astonish me!" Their calls of the wild answered, each singing pair will mate and deposit eggs for a new generation. Some, like the tree cricket, will bore into a soft stem and deposit eggs in its pith. The praying mantis, now three or four inches long with aging brown wings, will deposit hers in a capsule glued to a twig. The orchestra is on stage. Be silent and listen!

Autumn is the season when we become more aware of the arachnids with which we share our Eden: the spiders. They spin their webs year round, but in the fall dewdrops string along their delicate draperies like lanterns at a summer garden party and we can see them more easily.

One spider, quarter-size, fashioned a web outside our kitchen window, draping its silky threads top to bottom and halfway across in a four-foot square. It stationed itself dead center, on the alert. As we ate our lunch, we watched it dash down its web ladder, capture and devour its own lunch, a lesser creature on the wing who came too close. Then it scampered off, back to the center of the web. The next day a slightly smaller spider built a slightly smaller web outside our den window. Then one day, the webs are gone, except for tattered remnants. Did a bird come by and pick the spiders off for lunch?

We traveled to the Shenandoah Valley in late September. On the way home through a lifting fog we were amazed to see hundreds of spider web traps in the meadows along the roadside, all strung with dewdrops, all the same approximate twelve-inch diameter, all turned in exactly the same direction like miniature satellite dishes in the tall grass. Do spiders know from which direction insects come? Do they go by the wind direction? I might find those answers if I did some research, but I prefer just to hold that luminous vision of all those spiders tuned into breakfast along the highway.

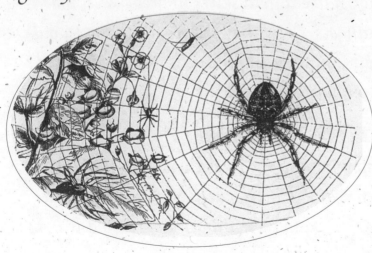

Rain Dance

First the wind came, like an orchestra tuning up, swaying the tree limbs this way and that, the leaves on their long, lacey green sleeves turning up their pale undersides like rolled-up cuffs. The swishing sound was a long sigh of joy, a wave of titters moving through a crowd: "O-ooh! A-aaaah!" Sighs of relief circulating like gossip, excitedly, through the forest. The leafy branches waved back and forth like taffeta skirts in great sweeping tangoes. Crows hawked from their lofty pulpits, announcing the news: "It's coming! It's coming!"

And the first drops fell. The frenetic waving stopped and the trees turned up their faces to the rain, drinking deep of the watery grace dripping to their thirsty limbs. And it lasted.

The peaceful drops fell steadily through he day, a tardy stop in a waning summer of blistering drought. Already many leaves of the great yellow tulip trees, Apollos of the forest, had fallen ending their season early, at least early by the way we reckon the calendar.

Some of our weathermen were wishing for a hurricane to fill our depleted reservoirs. Not I. Give me the sweet pit-pat of gentle all-day and all-night rain, the kind not strained, that falls like mercy on the earth below, to twist a metaphor from Shakespeare. And so it did, blessed rain.

Rain took a few reprises, light showers but welcomed, in the waning days of August before the season dried out again. Life was refreshed. No great trees fell. The grass greened up. The earth smells sweet. All will go on as before. Hope has been planted. The rainbow can wait. It rained!

Paean to a Mushroom

Mushroom Extraordinare! If there is one example of beauty coming from rot, it must be the luscious-looking fungi which sprout from the decaying logs of fallen trees.

Ours are growing on the detritus of fallen trees brought down by hurricane Floyd and other summer storms this year. One, outside our windows, looks like a giant beige velvet rose tinged with brown. It could be a bright new trim in the renaissance of last year's Easter bonnet or a saucy statement at the v-cut back of a granddaughter's prom dress. It is that lush and velvety. Except that day-by-day it has grown to the proportions of a dinner plate, enough to make a hat itself. "And why not?" I can almost hear some sprightly night-dancing wood nymph exclaim from

under its delicate brim. I've watched to see if nibbles occur around its fungus ears where some forest vole has tested if it might be edible. None so far. It does seem to be broadcasting an invitation to something; it is so flamboy-ant.

As quickly as it came after the damp rain 10 days ago, so daily the satiny beige of my tro-phy fungus begins to brown as if toasted by the sun and its pagoda-like leaves begin to shrivel at the edges in the dry air. But hope!

More rain is forecast. If I watch, I may see ever more overlapping convolutions fan out and ever more varied shades of beige swirl and bloom. "My mushroom" has a life of its own.

It's an Advent theme, this cycling out the old and fleshing out the new. A beginning again. This special millennium year also recalls the time of jubilee when the people of old marked the cycle of time in sevens and seven-times-seven, and let a year between the countings create change. A time to let the land lie fallow to rest and rejuvenate itself; a time to excuse debts, to set captives free, a time to make things right—and then to celebrate. Indeed, how visionary our forebears since Eden have been; their knowing, a knowing of earth; their unity, a unity with all things living and not living. They were one with the mountain, plain, and water. They watched the stars for signs and predictions and built monumental works to toll the cycles they read as movements of the sun and thus to plot their calendars, their feasts, and plant their crops. By these means they learned that, yes, the new season is always coming, that life is cyclical, but lasting.

There is no better teacher than the earth. We study its changes and often, more sadly, the effect we have upon it and how we live our lives on it. Meanwhile, we have the lesson of the lowly, but ever-so-lovely fungus to renew our faith in the ongoing-ness of creation.

Life prevails.

Palmetto Pause

A sojourn in South Carolina on the barrier island of Edisto offered an opportunity to live closely with nature in a different natural community. Edisto is a protected wetlands ecosystem. A Bermuda high lay over the area offering perfect dry, late summer days, a sapphire sky, and a cerulean blue Atlantic. Dunes bloomed with bright gaillardia and yellow aster, orange and yellow lantana, and other tiny mysteries. Endangered sea oats tickled the breeze, untouchable to us who walk there, as are—for other reasons—the spikey sand burr grasses.

No boardwalk, no stores, just neat painted cottages that leave the beach to the shells which pile up as the tide goes out. A few children and grandmothers glean them early before they bleach in the sun. Empty shells of horseshoe crabs are testament that gulls were here at dawn to clean them out for an early meal.

Edisto is one of the areas where loggerhead turtles beach themselves en masse and leave their eggs to incubate for two moon cycles. Locals mark the nests buried in the sand by flagging them to warn off trespassers. On late September nights hatchlings take their first baby steps to catch the surf which takes them out to their future ocean home. People who live near the beach keep their house lights turned off so as not to entice the tiny newborns ashore, instead of following the moonlight into the ocean. We missed that cavalcade, but followed a giant grandfather loggerhead in Big Bay between the beach and the mainland.

Great blue heron fished the lagoon behind our quarters along with the yellow-billed great white egret and the black-billed smaller egret. Double-breasted cormorants competed, swimming under water 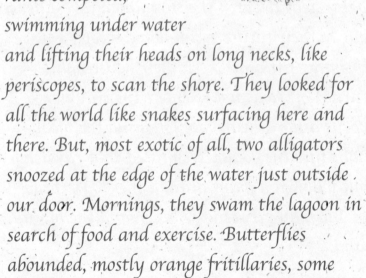 and lifting their heads on long necks, like periscopes, to scan the shore. They looked for all the world like snakes surfacing here and there. But, most exotic of all, two alligators snoozed at the edge of the water just outside our door. Mornings, they swam the lagoon in search of food and exercise. Butterflies abounded, mostly orange fritillaries, some sulphur yellows, and one (rare to me) yellow and black tiger-striped. Red dragonflies and purple iridescent damsel flies flitted incessantly in the sun, resting on sticks to lay their eggs.

And they all get along! "Our" lagoon was a real community. A lesson for us. Big or small, mighty or ephemeral, each has a fitting place, side by side with all the others, selecting its prey, competing with flair, but gamely. It was a lesson in living that we brought back to our community. And that day, it just happened, was Community Day.

Memory Woods

*I*t isn't a good day for people, but it is a good day for trees," the pastor noted at the ceremony dedicating the trees planted in memory of deceased neighbors. But, as it turned out, it was a good day for people, too. It was rainy and it was cold. But a tent had been raised over the chapel road and chairs set up. A hundred people sat closely together in that special intimacy that bearing bad weather brings. The rain felt entirely appropriate, dropping gently like Grace from the hands of the Creator of all things—of people and of trees—and reflecting the remembered tears of collected families and friends.

We planted one tree in memory of all those neighbors who have died before now, reminding ourselves that, though their memories share one tree, each was an individual and challenging us, the living, to continue our commitment to each other.

And then a rich contralto voice rose a cappella in harmony with the falling rain. The song was an original composition, created especially for the occasion, inspired by a line in the program inviting us to, "Walk among the trees."

Returning indoors, I consider how fortunate we are that we can literally walk among the treetops, along the bridges that connect our buildings. It is an advantage for sighting birds rarely seen at ground level. We spotted a true Baltimore Oriole (not the ones nesting in Camden Yards) in a paulownia tree.

Birds in our neighborhood live
with hazards and one of them
is the high level of these
bridges and of many of our windows.

A stunned scarlet tanager, fallen from
above, rested for most of a day on the
awning below our windows. Brilliant red with
jet black wings, he attracted the
attention of a nosey sparrow, who
danced around a bit and helplessly left his
friend to recover. Later in the day, I spied the
tanager perched on a dead branch in the
nearest American beech, surviving for another
day, I hope he is back in his aerial habitat
and nurturing fledglings.

Tomato Summer

I'm convinced. Plants do have emotions. In the play "The Effect of Gamma Rays on Man-in-the-Moon Marigolds" by Paul Dindel, a little girl talks to some plants; they thrive much better than those she ignores. I observe this on my kitchen windowsill. The temperamental potted "shamrock" visibly shivers with delight when I dribble water tenderly over its roots. It looks up at me and I'm sure it smiles and whispers a sybaritic sigh!

Michael Pollan has written in *The Botany of Desire* that a garden is: "... an oddly sociable, public sort of place, in which species seem eager to give one another the time of day; they dress up, flirt, flit, visit." And I say "Yes!"

The zinnias, marigolds, and salvia nestled in

the bed beside the mailroom were already a-
bloom in June, tossing their tufted hats into
the ring just as the dancing daylilies, flush
with the applause of garden-watchers, folded
their skirts and bowed out. Zinnias always
come on strong, decked out in sunny colors. A
florescent red one—it doesn't like to be called
fuschia which is not even a cousin plant-
wise—and a deep orange one know these are
the colors that our retinas pick up easiest in
the dark. And there are Joseph-coat shades in
between. There's the salvia, fire-engine red or
deep blue. The garden is orderly and bright
with bloom. Summer glory.

Out of the warming flower bed a stranger
poked its raggedy head. Just like last year,
another mystery guest. Last year, after weeks
of waiting—resisting calling it a weed—that
invader turned out to be a great Queen
Anne's lace. And I do mean "great." It was

five feet tall! Now, this new intruder looked for all the world—could it be? It is—a tomato plant! Where did it come from? To be sure "culprits" abound: birds, rabbits, squirrels? Lacking other suspects, that's the ticket! Papa squirrel raided somebody's vegetable patch and dropped the leavings at our door.

A week or two of commiseration followed the discovery of our uninvited guest. To pull it up felt too much like murder. The idea of moving it came full-face with the reality of no place else to put it. And so it stayed and grew, and grew, and GREW. It branched, and branched, and BRANCHED. We staked it with a twig, then a small branch. One day there was a bloom, then three or four. Bunches of small green tomatoes took their places as the blossoms faded. Resigned to the permanence of its residency, we staked it finally with a sturdy pole. Passersby kept a daily count as the fruits hung heavier and heavier on its branching arms. Soon there were too many to count.

So it was with the wild tomato plant that shot up like a teenager in the midst of our zinnias. The zinnias competed with cheerleader colors. Eager to outdo, in search of my attention, the tomato waved its arms in every direction. As I eased it into gentle braces, fashioned from spent daylily leaves, it wrapped itself around my neck and tousled my hair. I didn't think it would mind looking erect and better dressed and I persisted, lest it beach itself prostrate worshipping the sun. But no, it flailed and flapped its long green fingers about my neck and flicked my cheeks.

Flirting? Indeed! It tried to seduce me with that aromatic herbal bewitchery unique to its tomato kind. I must say it worked. I heard myself say out loud, "Oh, please!" as it wound a teasing bract around my arm, trying to woo me into its embrace. We came to terms. Compromised, it stood more beautiful against a pole, its daylily ties nearly invisible.

Beautiful and bountiful. Having won its place in our Eden, it did its part, producing luscious, plump red fruits in weighty clusters. So, it has flirted and hugged and been kissed by butterflies and fertilized by bees. And it has rewarded its caregivers with mouth-watering, sun-warmed, tart-sweet Maryland morsels of goodness.

Once, after a thorough drenching, the whole plant flopped dead-flat, sprawled on the ground like a fighter down for the count. "Give it up," some said, "it's broken and can't be saved." Doggedly, we lifted its ungainly arms, rammed the pole more firmly into the ground

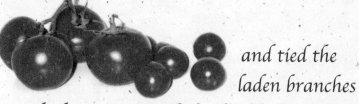 and tied the laden branches with the remnants of the daylily leaves half thinking the next day we would find it wilted and dying. But no, this plant was a fighter! It flourished and spread its arms every which way, filled like harvest baskets with plump green tomatoes. They hung in bunches, like grapes. Passersby began looking for touches of red. Would they ever…? Ah yes, as we sit here in mid-August, there is finally one tomato-red fruit.

Katherine Mansfield had her "Toothache Sunday;" I have had my "Tomato Summer." Before leaving for a trip to Italy, I reinforced the already strained ties on our renegade cherry tomato plant, resolved to put a little starch into its posture so it could hold its head up to the passing public while I was gone. I was proud of my summer of care and cultivation.

Italy was beautiful in late summer: vineyards heavy with ripening grapes, orchards hung with lemons. And along the famous Amalfi drive cherry tomato plants, red with fruit, hung over roadside walls. But sadly, to my eye, they lay sun-bleached, prone against the rocks, their leaves yellow and dying. "No problem," said our Italian friend, a grand-mother. "It is the way of it," she explained, the tomato plant actually being a vine, of course. It was then that I learned more respect for cherry tomatoes. They are the choice for the best tomato sauce. What's more, their flavor is greatly enhanced if the vine is watered only until it blooms and then is allowed to die in the sun as the tomatoes ripen. I had to admit, right then and there, that our tomato plant at home was a lot smarter than I! On the spot, I resolved to apologize and release my captive from its bonds.

After a fresh seafood pasta lunch in Amalfi (during which I learned that the best pasta is cooked in rain water!) we took a longer route back, returning by an interior road through the Appenines. A final exclamation point to my summer of tomato education came as we passed through Angra. The town produces the most tomato sauce in the whole world. Of course, they use cherry tomatoes, their flavor concentrated as they ripened in the Italian sun on yellowing water-starved vines.

I needn't have worried about the vine I left behind. I returned to find our tomato plant in its lounging mode again, stretching its leafy—albeit still green—branches every which way along the ground. I thought I heard a conde-scending snicker as I pulled away its already defeated shackles and let the vine fall lazily to the ground. "Okay, so you won," I said out loud when no one was looking. I had to admit it. The intruder had won.

Legacy

*"All Souls Day flowers on every grave are blowing.
Once in the year for all the dead a day."*

The words of this European art song reflect
the mood of All Soul's Day, commemorated on
November 2 in the Christian tradition. Even
during the time when the Berlin wall stood
between them, West German families were
permitted to pass through the Brandenburg
Gate on that day to place flowers on the
graves of loved ones in East Germany. Riding
through the Low Countries and northern
France one passes cemeteries a-bloom with
bright autumn bouquets, joyfully blowing
among the lichened gray tombs. In Mexico,
bright yellow marigolds decorate graves
throughout the countryside. "This is your
day," they are saying, "you are still with us."

The red, orange, yellow, and copper tones of our autumn leaves are the golden legacy of another year. Having lived out their natural Maryland year, they leave us an inheritance of beauty. Bright orange pumpkins, ripened in the womb of summer, enliven our celebration of the harvest and its baptism, Thanksgiving.

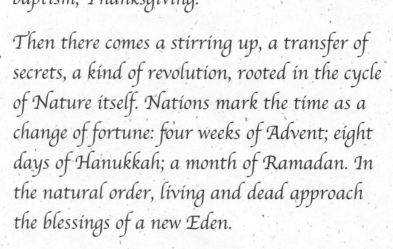

Then there comes a stirring up, a transfer of secrets, a kind of revolution, rooted in the cycle of Nature itself. Nations mark the time as a change of fortune: four weeks of Advent; eight days of Hanukkah; a month of Ramadan. In the natural order, living and dead approach the blessings of a new Eden.

It's the Berries

This time of year, it's the berries...an amazing variety! And thank goodness. There is life food in all those berries and the small wildlife and birds are surely grateful. Departing robins and resident starlings denuded what berries the dogwoods produced this dry year. The wineberry pantry is long since bare; the robins gobbled them in late summer. But small birds passing through or remaining here in winter can forage, if not feast, on many others: nandina, hawthorn, andromeda, tasty blue juniper, juicy red yew berries and, of course, holly.

Sparrows play hide-and-seek among the beauty berries. House finches raid the pyracantha. A squirrel bites off a whole bunch and scampers off with it. Mockingbirds move up and down the ivy climbing the trees outside our apartment.

Speaking of middle age, roses come to the autumn of life with plump hips. Birds find them luscious. Along the trail near the stream, a wild rose thicket becomes a thorny shelter with its cafeteria. In the deadest of winter feathered customers flit in and out. A great place to hang out. Chirping parties go on almost constantly.

All berries aren't nourishing. Some, like mistletoe, are toxic. Humans are allergic to some, like sumac, but winter resident birds, like cardinals and mockingbirds, devour them.

Berries are beautiful. Dusty grey bayberries decorate bare stems along the landscaped highway. Bright red bittersweet with its burst orange capsule climbs the steeps along the Patapsco River. Powder blue eucalyptus pods grace my kitchen shelf. These are the winter berries, the grandmothers of spring's seeds and summer's flowers, and the life-giving aunties of wintering-over birds and wildlife.

The Light of Autumn

From my perch here among the treetops I am awash in autumn light. The sun reflecting off the yellow leaves of our great tulip poplars bathes my rooms in glowing gold, a gouache my watercolor palette tries to capture.

The bright November day—nine years ago now—when we moved in, that light was a beacon of welcome. I set my houseplants in place on the wide sills. Now, a school of potted plants thrive at my corner windows including three pampered orchids. I can move them by season from eastern morning light in summer to southern day-long light in winter. They enjoy as much as I do the sybaritic pleasure in a change of scene. Every time I water them they say so!

When I have geraniums, a humming bird or

butterfly, even a bee, will approach the window pane attracted by the inviting red heads with their multiple sipping stations. I am still and they do not see me in their single-minded concentration. I think of Emily Dickinson's lines:

> "The bee is not afraid of me,
> I know the butterfly…"

Then, as quickly as they came, my visitors— or rather my geraniums' visitors—go below where we have planted scarlet salvia outdoors for their supping.

After dark we have the full moon of November, night light of autumn. Its magnetic attraction is real. It governs the tides. In its full phase it multiplies the surge that comes ashore in hurricanes. This same magnetism affects vegetation. Traditional farmers schedule plantings according to the phases of the moon: waxing, then full, then waning. In a humorous anecdote from our Eastern Shore, when asked by a young farmer, "On what moon do you plant your corn?" old farmer Reid replied, "I don't plant it on the moon, I plant it in the groun'."

The effect of the moon is a real phenomenon. Once we drove up into Big Thompson Canyon in Colorado during the full moon to observe moose and hear their bugling calls as they herded in an open field during their rutting season. In our awe at the primitive power of Nature thus to command its own survival, we "stayed too long at the ball" and had to spend the rest of the night in the shelter of a mountain chapel as the road closed behind us in an unexpected snow squall. After the experience "Shine on harvest moon for me and my gal," was less a romantic myth, we thought, and more a natural truth.

My Nature Notes

My Nature Notes

My Nature Notes

My Nature Notes

My Nature Notes

My Nature Notes

My Nature Notes

My Nature Notes